OYSTERS

John DeMers   Andrew Jaeger

CELESTIALARTS
Berkeley, California

CELESTIAL ARTS

P.O. Box 7123
Berkeley, California 94707

Distributed in Canada by Ten Speed Canada, in the United
Kingdom and Europe by Airlift Books, in New Zealand by
Southern Publishers Group, in Australia by Simon & Schuster
Australia, in South Africa by Real Books, and in Singapore,
Malaysia, Hong Kong, and Thailand by Berkeley Books.

Cover and interior design by Greene Design
Cover photograph by Michael Palumbo

Printed in Singapore

Library of Congress Catalog Card Number:
0-89087-869-2

1 2 3 4 5 6 7 8 9 10 / 08 07 06 05 04 03 02 01 00 99

⑥ INTRODUCTION ⑥

We'll never know who was the fabled "brave man" who first ate an oyster. But we do know that millions of oysters have been devoured ever since. All over the world, oysters have attracted a devoted following. In the United States, thousands of patriots have pledged their allegiance to the oyster, from the Hangtown Fry of San Francisco to the Peacemaker of New Orleans.

With the flavors of delicate French *claires,* rough but juicy *portugaises,* and exquisite *belons* still clinging to their taste buds, America's early gastronomic explorers must have been delighted to discover plump, salty oysters in bays and inlets all along the East Coast. They feasted on them in the eighteenth century, as we feast upon them now. We eat so many oysters, in fact, that Mother Nature can't keep up. Oysters must be carefully farmed and have been cultivated since the 1600s in our brackish bayous and salt marshes. Generally, shallow water bottoms are leased to oyster growers, who then seed their turf with "spat," an unromantic name for young oysters.

These oysters are eventually moved closer to salty waters, a process that gives the bivalves their characteristic flavor. In all, a typical oyster is moved four or five times before it's ready for market. If you've ever run into an oyster that's flat, flabby, and tasteless, you've probably run into one that somebody hustled for quick cash before its time.

This cultivated supply has been met with a steady demand. Oldtimers recall there were once oyster bars all over coastal cities, ramshackle havens where you could step out of the sun and knock back raw oysters for about a dime a dozen. Sadly, nearly all of these traditional oyster bars have gone the way of the free lunch.

Throughout the twentieth century, American chefs have built many dishes around oysters. More than a few lists of best dishes converge on things like broiled oysters with pasta, oysters bordelaise, or fried oysters on spinach with melted Brie. Yet in a sense, all this opening, frying, souping, sautéing, saucing, and panéeing only brings us to the threshold of America's single most famous contribution to the world of oyster cookery—baked oyster dishes.

Since 1899, these dishes have grabbed a special place in our hearts, and they've never even hinted they might let go. The idea of topping fresh oysters with some mixture of seafoods, seasonings, and sauces, then baking them till they're crusty and brown, has over the years become a food category unto itself. Frying also plays a role in the oyster's popularity, so great attention is paid to avoiding the pitfalls of that technique. And any paean to the oyster would be incomplete if it failed to mention the New Orleans oyster loaf. In a sense, this is only a variation on the ubiquitous fried oyster "po'boy," only with a much better story. Among the nineteenth-century Creoles, the oyster loaf was known as the "mediatrice," or peacemaker. Whenever a gentleman would have a spat with his wife (and in this case, "spat" didn't mean young oysters), he would bring her an oyster loaf in hopes of appeasement. Apparently, it worked a lot better than flowers or chocolates.

All over the United States, from spartan bars and sandwich shops to the loftiest outlets of *haute* cuisine, the oyster is reigning once again. In fact, we might go so far as to say, everytime it rains, it rains oysters from heaven!

Chefs never seem to tire of playing off the oyster classics—occasionally farther off than many diners wish. Through it all, the valiant oyster has shown itself to have a sense of humor, tolerating a barrage of abuses in order to stumble on the occasional moment of glory.

HOW TO OPEN AN OYSTER

Prying open an oyster can be one of the more dangerous things you do in your life. But with practice and plenty of care, the business can become safe and satisfying.

Start by watching a professional at an oyster bar. The pros usually use a heavy lead anvil shaped like an S to hold the shell in place, plus a so-called oyster knife that's notable for the fact that a nuclear attack probably couldn't break off its blade. However, you don't really need either of these, but you do need to be careful to avoid giving yourself a deep and painful cut.

You may use an oyster knife, a strong screwdriver with a paring knife on the side, or even one of those old-fashioned can openers that make a triangular hole. Hold the oyster securely in one hand, then pry the oyster open at the hinge just enough to be able to slip in the blade of the paring knife and sever the adductor muscle that connects to the two halves of the shell. This should allow the top shell to lift right off.

Next, slip the blade under the oyster itself and cut the second half of the muscle. You should sequence your work so it always leaves the oyster on the deeper half of shell, giving it a bed it's unlikely to slide off of. And be sure to preserve every drop of the liquid (called oyster water or oyster liquid), by opening oysters over a bowl (once you're skilled enough). Also remember to set aside the oyster shells for use in presentation.

Use your knife to scrape off any bitter-tasting dark mud that has lodged where the two hinges were joined together, and also check for any tiny pieces of shell that may be on the oyster.

A MENU GUIDE TO OYSTERS

Oysters are classified scientifically by only a handful of Latin names, but marketed under a wide variety of romantic monikers, most having to do with their place of origin.

For instance, most oysters enjoyed along the Atlantic and Gulf coasts are officially *Crassostrea virginica*—all mild in flavor, though ranging considerably in saltiness. But just try telling someone in Bristol, Maine, that his oysters are the same species as those taken from the bay in Apalachicola, Florida. You may well have a food fight on your hands.

Pride may lurk behind most of these fisticuffs, but there is also a little bit of epicurean good sense. An oyster's development is dictated by its species, with certain characteristics notable in all possible siblings. Yet they also draw taste and texture from their environment. Tides, water salinity, the presence of food, and algae all play a role in what an oyster is like as food.

Chefs in America these days like to describe every cherry or kumquat on the plate in terms of where it hails from, so here's an alphabetical user's guide to some of the most important oysters from some of the most important oyster places.

APALACHICOLA: You can spot these famed Florida natives by their rounded green shell and their deep cup. Fans throughout the Panhandle describe their flavor as mild and slightly sweet. Species: *Crassostrea virginica.*

BLUEPOINT: When you read this word on a menu today, you're reading more history than current events. Bluepoint refers to any mild Atlantic oyster, long after the bivalves from New York's Blue Point on Great South Bay have ceased to be in production. Species: *Crassostrea virginica.*

CHESAPEAKE BAY: Here's a clear reference to the seafood-blessed bay shared by Maryland, Virginia, and Delaware, as well as broadly to the accompanying cuisine some have dubbed DelMarVa. The round shell with a small cup takes you inside for a mild, sweet treat. Species: *Crassostrea virginica.*

CHINCOTEAGUE: Another, smaller bay shared by Maryland and Virginia produces a slightly different tasting oyster, this one with a distinctive aftertaste. The shell is round and flat. Species: *Crassostrea virginica.*

EUROPEAN FLAT: Here's an oyster you run into sometimes, usually under the name belon. Originally from Brittany, they are revered by oyster lovers around the world. Belons are now raised along coldwater coasts in Maine and Washington. Species: *Ostrea edulis.*

GOOSE POINT: This is a specific part of Willapa Bay in Washington. And this specific point produces a specific oyster, with reddish highlights marking its deeply cupped shell. Species: *Crassostrea gigas.*

KUMAMOTO: Epicures love its buttery texture, as well as its not-so-salty, almost fruity flavor. It's found in waters from British Columbia to Mexico. Species: *Crassostrea gigas.*

LOUISIANA GULF: These populist heroes come from the bays and bayous strewn throughout the

Mississippi River Delta. Their thick shells give way to very plump meat admired for its soft, almost fatty texture. Louisiana oysters have a mildly salty flavor, though the locals all say: The saltier the better. Species: *Crassostrea virginica*.

MALPEQUE: These small oysters from Prince Edward Island in Canada are slightly bitter. Their shells are pointed and oblong, and their flesh has a firm texture and a clean aftertaste. Species: *Crassostrea virginica*.

OLYMPIA: These tiny oysters used to grow wild along the Pacific Coast from Alaska to California. Today, the small North American type is raised in Puget Sound, Washington, and Humbolt Bay, California. Enthusiasts speak of its mild coppery aftertaste. Species: *Ostrea lurida*.

QUILCINE: These natives of the Quilcine bay in Washington are known for their flavor, which blends mildly salty with subtly sweet. Their aftertaste is sometimes compared to cucumber. Species: *Crassostrea gigas*.

WELLFLEET: One of Atlantic Coast's most prestigious bivalves, these contenders from Cape Cod tend to be small, with a moderately salty and clean taste. Species: *Crassostrea virginica*.

WILLAPA BAY: A great name to know in menu language these days, Willapas hail from Washington. They come from a deeply cupped, multi-hued shell and are described as plump and full of both salty and sweet flavor accents. Species: *Crassostrea gigas*.

BEFORE SWINE

This recipe just in: Boned Oysters from Charles of Myteline on the Greek isle of Lesbos, 3rd century.

Use only the large Asiatic oysters caught in the Indian Ocean, Black Sea, or the Persian and Arabian Gulfs. Use the delicious white meat only. Discard the large white bone sometimes discovered inside the shell — or give it to a passing Persian. They seem to prefer these bones to gold; they call them 'pearls.'

CONTENTS

Creole Seasoning

In New Orleans, we use this spice blend instead of basic salt and pepper. You'll find it gives a nice zip to almost any dish.

5 tablespoons paprika
1 tablespoon ground black pepper
1 tablespoon ground red pepper
1 tablespoon ground white pepper
1 tablespoon dried crushed thyme
2 tablespoons garlic powder
1 tablespoon ground oregano
1 teaspoon salt
1 teaspoon chili powder
1 teaspoon onion powder

In a small bowl, blend all the spices with a whisk.

Makes about 1 cup

Egg Wash

Some of our dishes employ this simple liquid mixture as part of a multi-step coating process. Be sure to follow the recipe closely, since dipping in egg wash produces different results depending on the sequence.

1 egg
2 cups milk
1/4 cup all-purpose flour

⑥ In a medium bowl, beat all ingredients together until smooth and incorporated.

Makes about 3 cups

'WITH NEARLY ALL SHELLS REPORTING'

The ancient Greeks actually cast votes using oyster shells as ballots. Each voter inscribed his choice of candidate on the soft mother-of-pearl interior, scratching the chosen name with a sharp point.

Jalapeño Tartar Sauce

If you think tartar sauce is boring by definition, don't give up until you've tried this variation the next time you're having a party.

2 finely chopped jalapeños
3/4 cup dill pickle relish
1/4 cup chopped white onions
1 quart mayonnaise

🍥 Mix together all ingredients in a large bowl. Refrigerate until chilled, at least 1 hour.

Makes about 1 1/2 cups

Remoulade Sauce

Much more pungent than the French sauce of the same name, this one makes seafood terrific—and clears your sinuses at the same time.

1/2 cup mayonnaise
1/2 cup Creole mustard or other coarse
    brown mustard
1 teaspoon white wine
1 dash Tabasco
1/2 cup paprika
2 anchovy fillets
1/2 tablespoon fresh lemon juice

🐚 Place 2 anchovy fillets in a medium bowl and mix with lemon juice. Mash until a paste is formed and add remaining ingredients. Mix well. Cover and refrigerate for 3 hours.

Makes about 1 cup

Cocktail Sauce

No exotic alternatives can replace this American classic when you're enjoying raw oysters or other chilled seafoods.

1 cup ketchup
1 tablespoon horseradish
1 teaspoon lemon juice
1 teaspoon Worcestershire sauce
1/4 teaspoon Tabasco sauce
Pinch of chili powder

Mix all the ingredients together in a small bowl.

Makes 1 cup

Lemon Ketchup

Both lemon juice and lemon zest make this sauce the simplest route to great taste with oysters.

1 cup ketchup
1 teaspoon lemon zest
1 teaspoon lemon juice

⑥ Mix ingredients together in a small bowl. Allow flavors to blend in the refrigerator for several hours.

Makes 1 cup

Oyster Cocktail

Here's a wonderful combination: cold, salty raw oysters with a tangy cocktail sauce. You may prefer a particular sauce, but don't decide for sure until you've tried this recipe.

1 head of lettuce, shredded
1 cup Cocktail Sauce (see below)
24 shucked oysters
2 lemons, quartered

COCKTAIL SAUCE:

1 cup ketchup
1 tablespoon horseradish
1 teaspoon lemon juice
1 teaspoon Worcestershire sauce
1/4 teaspoon Tabasco sauce
2 pinches of chili powder

⑥ Mix ingredients for cocktail sauce together in a medium bowl and set aside.

Divide lettuce equally on 4 salad plates. Top with 6 oysters each. Cover oysters with 1/4 cup cocktail sauce. Garnish each plate with 2 lemon wedges.

Makes 4 servings (6 oysters each)

EAST IS EAST

Oysters are a vital part of several Asian cuisines. Hong Kong and the Philippines are famous for bivalves growing to a size of nine inches (Crassostrea gigas); these are always cooked before eating. In Hong Kong they are often sun-dried. The more commonly devoured oysters in Asia are Saccostrea cucullata and Crassostrea cucullata, eaten both cooked and raw.

Oyster Shooters

It's hard to imagine getting bored with fresh oysters on the half-shell. But these oysters in a shot glass have developed their fan club too.

1 cup cocktail sauce (see page 20)
1 cup Bloody Mary mix
16 shucked oysters

⑥ Mix cocktail sauce and Bloody Mary mix together in a medium bowl. Place oysters in a shot glass with 2 tablespoons (1 ounce) of sauce. Serve with lemon wedges. Shoot as you would Schnapps.

Serves 4 (4 shooters each)

Oysters with Lemon Ketchup

If you prefer a dipping sauce that's not too spicy, consider this simple mixture of two tastes that are perfect with oysters—ketchup and lemon.

1 head of lettuce, shredded
1 cup Lemon Ketchup (see page 23)
24 shucked oysters
2 lemons, quartered

Ⓖ Divide lettuce equally on 4 salad plates. Top with 6 oysters each. Cover oysters with 1/4 cup lemon ketchup. Garnish each plate with 2 lemon wedges.

Makes 4 servings (6 oysters each)

Oysters with Fresh Salsa

There are lots of things that taste great with this fresh Southwestern salsa. Suffice it to say that raw oysters are at or near the top of our list.

1 head of lettuce, shredded
1 cup salsa (see below)
24 shucked oysters
2 lime wedges, quartered

SALSA:
1 cup finely chopped tomatoes
2 tablespoons finely chopped green onions
1 teaspoon chopped fresh garlic
1 teaspoon finely chopped fresh cilantro
1 tablespoon fresh lemon juice
1 tablespoon coarsely ground black pepper
1 tablespoon freshly chopped jalapeño pepper
1 cup Bloody Mary mix

⑥ Combine salsa ingredients in a mixing bowl.

Divide lettuce equally on 4 salad plates. Top with 6 oysters each. Cover oysters with 1/4 cup salsa. Garnish each plate with 2 lime wedges.

Makes 4 servings

FOUR-LEGGED FIEND

The coon oyster of Florida once grew abundantly in that state's mangroves. Tragically, its growth was seriously stunted by the relentless predation of raccoons — who, like Samuel Johnson's legendary cat, were oyster-eating machines on four legs. The coon oyster was considered similar in flavor to the small, delicate chipi chipi found in Venezuela.

Oyster Chowder

While the Gulf Coast is a long way from the famous chowder country in New England, we have our own version using not only oysters, but also shrimp and crawfish. We'll stake our chowder against theirs any day.

1/4 pound (1 stick) butter

1 cup diced onions

1 cup diced celery

1 cup diced bell peppers

2 cups diced potatoes

8 cups chicken or fish stock

1/2 pound shucked oysters

1/4 pound crawfish tail meat

1/4 pound shrimp (50-60 count), peeled and deveined

1 cup whole kernel corn

1/2 cup oyster water

1/4 cup finely sliced green onions

1/8 cup Worcestershire sauce

1/2 tablespoon black pepper

1/2 teaspoon thyme

1/4 teaspoon cayenne pepper

1/4 cup all-purpose flour

1 cup cold water

⑥ In a large stockpot, sauté butter, onions, celery, and bell peppers. Add diced potatoes and chicken stock or fish stock and bring to a boil. Add remaining ingredients except for the flour. Return to a boil.

In a separate bowl, mix flour with 1 cup cold water. Stir into the chowder to thicken. Serve with warm crusty French bread.

Makes 10 to 12 servings

Oyster &
Artichoke Soup

*Unlike most classic New Orleans dishes,
this modern tradition has a living, breathing
creator—the great chef Warren LeRuth.
Today, his silky soup is served all over
the place.*

1 tablespoon melted butter
1 tablespoon all-purpose flour
1 cup milk
1/2 cup heavy cream
1/2 cup quartered artichoke hearts
1/4 cup oyster water or clam juice
1 dozen shucked oysters
1/2 teaspoon salt
1/4 teaspoon white pepper
1/4 tablespoon parsley
1/4 teaspoon tarragon
Tabasco sauce

⑥ In a medium stockpot, stir flour into melted butter and whisk together. Over medium heat, add milk and whisk until thick. Add remaining ingredients. Heat until broth thickens and oysters curl, about 6 to 7 minutes. Add 2 teaspoons of Tabasco just before serving.

Serves 2

Oyster Bisque

While this is a fairly universal thickened oyster soup, the use of the roux as thickener helps tie it to the Creoles and Cajuns of south Louisiana.

1/2 pound (2 sticks) butter
1 cup all-purpose flour
1 cup diced onions
1 cup diced green bell peppers
1 cup diced celery
2 tablespoons parsley
2 tablespoons diced green onions
6 cups oyster water or clam juice
1 teaspoon coarsely ground black pepper
1/4 teaspoon salt
1 bay leaf
1/4 cup sherry
1 tablespoon Tabasco sauce
1 tablespoon Worcestershire sauce
1/2 cup heavy cream
36 shucked oysters
1/2 cup finely chopped green onions

⑥ In a medium stockpot, melt butter over medium heat. Whisk in flour. Continue whisking over high heat until mixture turns medium beige in color, about 6 minutes. Stir in onions, peppers, celery, parsley, and 2 tablespoons green onion. Add oyster water, pepper, salt, bay leaf, sherry, Tabasco, and Worcestershire sauce. Cover pot and bring to boil for 2 minutes. Add heavy cream. Boil for 8 minutes. Press the stock through a sieve into a large bowl and then return to the stockpot and bring to a boil. Add oysters and 1/2 cup chopped green onions. Season with salt to taste. Simmer over low heat until oysters curl, 2 to 3 minutes.

Serves 10 to 12

Oyster
Brie Soup

*Combine the classic French cheese with
a cream-based oyster soup and you have a
warming, elegant dinner. For an extra treat,
place a slice of thick, crusty French bread
across the top, as you might do with onion
soup. C'est magnifique!*

1/4 pound (1 stick) butter
1/4 cup all-purpose flour
8 ounces brie, rind removed
2 cups milk
1 cup oyster water
1 cup heavy cream
1 cup white wine
2 teaspoons Tabasco sauce
1/4 teaspoon salt
1/2 teaspoon coarsely ground black pepper
18 shucked oysters
2 tablespoons finely chopped green onions
1/4 teaspoon tarragon

⑥ In a medium saucepan, melt butter over medium heat. Whisk in flour. Add brie, milk, oyster water, cream, and wine. Stir constantly until cheese is melted. Add Tabasco, salt, and pepper. Bring to a boil. Add oysters, green onion, and tarragon. Cook until oysters curl, 4 to 5 minutes.

Serves 4

LOVE IS IN THE SHELL

It's not entirely clear how oysters came to be championed as aphrodisiacs, since science has uncovered little to support such claims. In many cultures it is believed that the oyster is as potent as powdered rhinoceros horn, but most aficionados would say oysters taste a lot better. It is known that Casanova downed 50 or more salty ones before heading out for each evening's conquest.

Oysters in Lobster Sauce

With its blend of soy and fermented black beans, this brothy spinoff on oysters and lobster is an Asian-inspired meal in itself.

STOCK:

8 cups water

1 whole lobster (1 pound)

1 lemon, halved

1 cup chopped onions

1 cup chopped celery

2 bay leaves

OYSTERS:

12-14 shucked oysters

1 egg

1/4 cup cold water

2 tablespoons cornstarch

2 tablespoons fermented black beans, rinsed and mashed with fork

2 tablespoons finely chopped green onions

2 tablespoons soy sauce

⑥ In a large stockpot, bring water to a boil. Add lobster, lemon, onions, celery, and bay leaves. Cover and boil for 10 minutes. Remove lobster. Remove the meat and set aside. Return the shells to the stockpot. Continue to boil until the stock is reduced to 2 cups, about 10 to 12 minutes. Strain and reserve.

Chop lobster meat into 1/2-inch pieces. Set aside.

Beat 1 egg in a cup until frothy. Set aside.

Dissolve corn starch in cold water. Set aside.

Add the lobster and the oysters to boiling stock. Cook until they curl, 3 to 4 minutes. Pour beaten egg into the boiling stock through the steam. Add the black beans, green onions, and soy sauce. Heat for 2 to 3 minutes.

Serves 4 to 6

Oysters Bienville

Count Arnaud of Arnaud's in New Orleans' French Quarter gave the world this baked oyster classic, probably sometime in the 1930s. We're sure you'll love it.

STOCK:

1 cup water
1/4 pound shrimp, peeled and deveined
1/4 cup chopped mushrooms
1/4 cup chopped celery
1/4 cup chopped onions
1 teaspoon chopped garlic
1/2 teaspoon salt
1/8 teaspoon black pepper
1/8 teaspoon Creole Seasoning (see page 16)

SAUCE:

2 tablespoons butter

1/4 cup flour

4 tablespoons white wine

4 tablespoons sherry

Reserved stock

3/4 cup heavy cream

1/4 cup water

3/4 cup grated Romano cheese

1/2 cup grated Cheddar cheese

1/4 cup finely sliced green onions

1/4 teaspoon red pepper flakes

1/2 teaspoon Crystal hot sauce

Dash Tabasco sauce

OYSTERS:

12 shucked oysters

1/4 cup water

2 tablespoons breadcrumbs

⑥ In a medium saucepan, combine stock ingredients. Cook over medium heat until the shrimp turn pink. Drain and reserve stock. In a food processor, purée all drained ingredients and set aside.

In a medium saucepan, melt butter, then whisk in flour. Add the white wine and the sherry, the reserved stock, and mix well. Add the cream and the water and bring to a boil. Whisk in cheeses, green onions, red pepper flakes, and hot sauces.

Preheat broiler.

In a medium saucepan, poach oysters in water until they curl. Place 6 oysters each into 2 medium ramekins. Cover each with sauce. Sprinkle each with 1 tablespoon of breadcrumbs. Broil at high until brown, 5 to 6 minutes. Serve hot.

Serves 2

Oysters Rockefeller

The recipe for Oysters Rockefeller was invented around 1900 by the good folks at Antoine's Restaurant, in the French Quarter, who declared the topping "rich enough for Rockefeller."

12 to 15 oysters on the half shell
1/2 cup water
1 teaspoon salt

PRODUCTION NUMBERS

The United States leads the world in oyster production, with the traditionally strongest area being Maryland on Chesapeake Bay. Next in terms of production comes Japan, then France, Denmark, the Netherlands, and Canada.

ROCKEFELLER SAUCE:

2 tablespoons butter

1 cup chopped fresh spinach

1 cup chopped turnip greens

1 cup chopped green onions

1 cup chopped green bell peppers

1 cup chopped celery

1 cup chopped white onions

1 cup chopped parsley

1 tablespoon chopped garlic

2 cups oyster water, reserved from shucking

1 cup shucked oysters

1 teaspoon lemon zest

2/3 cup freshly grated pecorino Romano cheese

2 tablespoons Pernod

2 teaspoons coarsely ground black pepper

1 teaspoon salt

1 teaspoon Tabasco sauce

4 lemon wedges, as garnish

⑥ Place the oysters in 1/2 cup water with a teaspoon of salt, simmer over medium heat until the edges start to curl, then remove with a slotted spoon. Discard the poaching liquid.

To prepare the sauce, melt the butter in a large pan. Add the vegetables, parsley, and garlic, and sauté until the vegetables ar soft and translucent, 8 to 10 minutes. Add the oyster water, oysters, and lemon zest, reducing over medium heat until the liquid is almost gone. Add the remaining ingredients for the sauce for the sauce and transfer to a blender. Blend to form a smooth paste.

Preheat the oven to 400°F.

Spoon the oyster mixture over the oysters on the half shell, molding with your hands. Set the oysters on a baking sheet and bake until the tops start to bubble and brown, about 5 minutes. Set on small plates, 3 or 4 oysters per person. Serve with lemon wedges.

Serves 4

Baked Garlic Oysters

Just about everywhere Sicilian immigrants settled around the turn of the century, they gave local seafood a treatment similar to this. Nothing else, however, works quite as well as oysters.

GARLIC OIL:

1 cup olive oil

5 tablespoons chopped garlic

1 tablespoon coarsely ground black pepper

1 tablespoon chopped parsley

1 tablespoon chopped green onions

16 shucked oysters

⑥ In a small bowl, mix garlic oil ingredients. Allow to sit at room temperature for 1 hour.

Preheat oven to 375°F.

Place oysters on half shell on baking pan. Place 1/4 teaspoon garlic oil on each oyster. Bake at 375°F for 10 minutes. Remove from the oven. Top each oyster with 1 teaspoon garlic oil. Return to the oven for 8 minutes. Spoon the remaining garlic oil over oysters.

Serves 4

Oyster Fritters

The act of making fritters propels us into the heart of the Caribbean, where islanders have been feasting on conch fritters for generations. We like the conch version, but we relish this oyster variation even more.

3 cups flour
1 1/2 cups corn flour
2 tablespoons sugar
1 tablespoon salt
1 tablespoon baking powder
1 cup shucked oysters, chopped
1/2 cup melted butter
1/4 cup milk
1/4 cup oyster water or clam juice
4 tablespoons thinly sliced green onions
3 tablespoons chopped parsley
1 tablespoon powdered garlic
1 teaspoon crushed red pepper flakes
1 teaspoon coarsely ground black pepper
Vegetable oil, for frying

⑥ In a large mixing bowl, first combine flours, sugar, salt and baking powder. Add oysters and liquid ingredients and combine. Add seasonings. Refrigerate for 30 minutes.

In a large skillet or frying pan, heat oil to 350°F.

Drop oyster mixture by tablespoons into the oil and fry for 3 to 4 minutes, until golden brown. Drain on paper towels and serve warm with your favorite sauce.

Makes 40 fritters

Jamaican Oysters

There are several Jamaican jerk seasonings available commercially, but we prefer to mix our own according to this recipe. The result is a baked oyster dish with echoes of the islands.

24 shucked oysters

MARINADE SAUCE:

1 cup white vinegar

1/4 cup orange juice

1/4 cup soy sauce

2 tablespoons lime juice

1 habanero pepper, quartered

2 tablespoons butter

JERK SPICE MIX:

1/2 cup ground allspice

1 tablespoon powdered garlic

1/2 tablespoon sugar

1/2 tablespoon thyme leaves

1/2 teaspoon cayenne pepper

1/4 teaspoon nutmeg

1/4 teaspoon cinnamon

⑥ Combine all marinade ingredients except butter in a medium bowl. Add oysters to the marinade. Cover and place in the refrigerator for 4 to 6 hours.

Mix jerk ingredients in a small bowl. Set aside.

Remove peppers from the marinade. Transfer 1 cup of marinade and the oysters to a medium saucepan. Poach oysters over medium heat until they curl for 4 to 5 minutes. Transfer each oyster to a clean oyster shell on a baking tray.

Preheat oven to 350°F. Simmer marinade over medium heat until sauce is reduced by half. Add butter and stir. Sprinkle each oyster with 1/4 teaspoon of Jerk Spice mix and 1 teaspoon of sauce.

Bake oysters in a preheated oven for 2 to 3 minutes to reheat.

Serves 10 to 12 as an appetizer

Oysters Jaeger

The oysters that carry our family name are more in honor of my Sicilian mother than my German father. No matter where your parents come from, you (and they) will love these.

16 oysters
4 strips uncooked, thinly sliced bacon
1/2 cup seasoned breadcrumbs
Grated Romano cheese

⑥ Preheat oven to 350°F.

Open oysters. Spread the half shells on a baking pan. Slice bacon into thin slices. Divide the bacon evenly on top of the oysters. Bake for 10 minutes. Remove from the oven. Top each oyster with breadcrumbs and cheese. Return to the oven for 8 minutes. Serve hot.

Serves 8 as an appetizer, 4 as an entrée

Fried Oysters Wrapped in Bacon

*Fried oysters are great all by themselves,
but this variation weaves the flavor of bacon
into the mix.*

6 slices of bacon, sliced in half
12 shucked oysters
1 cup cornmeal seasoned with salt and pepper
1 cup egg wash (see page 17)
Oil for frying

⑥ Wrap each oyster with 1/2 piece of bacon. Seal
with a toothpick. Dip each wrapped oyster in egg
wash, then cornmeal. Heat oil in a skillet to 350°F.
Fry oysters until golden brown, 3 to 5 minutes.

Serves 6 as an appetizer, 4 as an entrée

Oysters Rumaki

We've always enjoyed the Asian dish served in this country as rumaki. But we've never tasted a dipping sauce quite as good as the one we're sharing here.

1 (5-ounce) can water chestnuts, rinsed and
   drained (16 to 20) water chestnuts
16 to 20 shucked medium oysters, 1 for each
   chestnut
8 to 10 strips of bacon, 1 for each 2 chestnuts

DIPPING SAUCE:

1 cup ketchup
1 teaspoon soy sauce
1 teaspoon honey
1 teaspoon chili paste
1/2 teaspoon seasoned rice vinegar

⑥ Combine ingredients for Dipping Sauce in a small bowl and set aside.

Preheat oven to 350°F.

Place oyster on top of a water chestnut. Wrap with 1/2 slice bacon and secure with a toothpick. Arrange on a baking sheet. Bake for 10 to 12 minutes. Serve hot.

Serves 8 as an appetizer, 4 as an entrée

AND WHAT'S YOUR SIGN?

Proximity to fresh water is a major factor in the flavor and sometimes even the color of an oyster, since oysters are vegetarians. Oysters process up to 25 gallons of water every 24 hours, consuming along the way minute plants known as diatoms. These bring to the oyster such minerals as copper, iron, and iodine.

Oyster with Pancetta and Pignoli

Two wonderful Italian sidekicks—the ham called pancetta and the pine nuts known as pignoli—lift this dish right into the stratosphere.

2 tablespoons pine nuts
1 tablespoon olive oil
2 tablespoons finely chopped pancetta
10 kalamata olives, pitted
6 quarters artichoke hearts
2 tablespoons finely chopped Roma tomatoes
12 shucked oysters
1 tablespoon rinsed capers
1/2 cup white wine
2 tablespoons butter
8 ounces pasta, cooked
2 tablespoons fresh parsley
1 tablespoon finely sliced green onions
1 tablespoon coarsely ground black pepper

⑥ In a medium saucepan, over high heat, toast pine nuts for 2 minutes, or until brown. Add the olive oil and pancetta and sauté until pancetta begins to crisp. Add olives, artichoke hearts, tomatoes, oysters, and capers, and continue to sauté until oysters curl. Add wine and bring to a boil. Lower heat and continue to cook about another 2 minutes, or until it has reduced by one third. Then cream in the butter. Remove from heat. Add the pasta, parsley, green onions, and pepper and toss. Serve warm.

Serves 2

Pasta
with Oysters

*Pasta is always great... but it's even greater
when tossed with oysters.*

2 tablespoons extra virgin olive oil
1 tablespoon garlic, chopped
1 cup chopped onions
1 tablespoon tomato paste
1 cup white wine
3 cups tomato sauce
2 cups chopped tomatoes
2 cups oyster water (or 1 cup bottled clam juice)
1 tablespoon oregano
1 tablespoon Worcestershire sauce
1 teaspoon coarsely ground black pepper
1/2 teaspoon Tabasco sauce
1 cup shucked oyster meat
1 cup green onions, chopped
1 tablespoon chopped fresh parsley
1 teaspoon sugar
8 ounces cooked pasta
Salt and pepper to taste
3 tablespoons grated Romano cheese

⑥ In a skillet, heat oil over medium heat. Add garlic and sauté for one minute. Add onions and cook until translucent. Add tomato paste and cook an additional 2 minutes. Add 1/4 cup wine and mix thoroughly. Add tomato sauce and chopped tomatoes. Cook 2 more minutes. Add remaining 3/4 cup wine and increase heat to light boil. Add oyster water or clam juice and bring to a boil. Continue to cook for 10 minutes or until reduced by one half. Add oregano, pepper, Tabasco, sugar, and Worcestershire. Reduce heat to a simmer and add oyster meat, green onions and parsley. Cook for about 20 minutes. Remove from heat.

In a large serving bowl, toss with pasta, season to taste, and top with freshly grated Romano cheese.

Serves 4 as an appetizer

Oyster Bruschetta

We're pleased by the number of restaurants that have taken to serving this olive oil drizzled, rustic grilled bread as a prelude to meals. We think people would order bruschetta as an entrée if it always came with oysters.

6 slices French bread, cut at an angle
4 tablespoons olive oil
1 tablespoon minced garlic
1 tablespoon freshly chopped parsley
1 teaspoon coarsely ground black pepper
6 slices prosciutto
18 shucked oysters
6 slices mozzarella cheese

⑥ Preheat oven to 375°F.

Combine olive oil, garlic, parsley, and pepper in a small mixing bowl. Brush each bread slice with the mixture on both sides and arrange on a baking sheet. Place 1 slice of prosciutto on each slice of bread and top each with 3 oysters.

Bake for 15 minutes. Top each piece with a slice of the mozzarella and return to the oven to melt the cheese. Serve hot.

Makes 6 bruschettas

Open-Faced Oyster Sandwiches with Blue Cheese Crumble

This is a newer creation of ours, and as often happens in our recipes, we take something familiar—in this case, fried oysters—and carry them someplace they've never been before.

4 strips bacon

SAUCE:

1 tablespoon melted butter

1/2 cup blue cheese, plus extra for topping

1/2 cup heavy whipping cream

1 1/2 teaspoons chopped fresh parsley

1/2 teaspoon Tabasco sauce

1 tablespoon olive oil

1 cup fresh spinach

4 large slices fresh bread, toasted

16 Fried Oysters (page 51)

⑥ In a large pan over medium heat, sauté the bacon until crisp, drain on paper towels, and crumble. Set aside.

In a medium saucepan, add all of the ingredients for the sauce. Whisk the mixture together over medium heat until it boils. Remove from heat.

In a small saucepan, heat the olive oil and sauté the spinach just until it starts to wilt, 3 to 4 minutes. Remove the pan from heat.

To assemble, place the spinach on the toasted bread on 4 small plates. Top each slice with 4 oysters, spoon some of the sauce over the oysters and bread, and sprinkle some of the bacon and blue cheese over the sauce. Serve immediately.

Serves 4

Oyster
Patties

It's hard to think of "party food" in New Orleans without thinking of oyster patties. Here's a safe bet to make your parties memorable.

1/2 cup melted butter
1/2 cup all-purpose flour
4 cups oyster water or clam juice
Pinch of cayenne pepper
1/2 teaspoon salt
1/2 teaspoon freshly ground black pepper
24 shucked oysters
1/2 cup chopped onions
1/2 cup chopped button mushrooms
2 tablespoons chopped fresh parsley
1 cup milk
1 cup heavy whipping cream
Dash of Tabasco sauce
1 sheet puff pastry dough

⑥ Make a light blond roux by combining the butter and flour and place in a large bowl. Add the oyster water, cayenne, salt, and pepper to form a broth. Set aside. Poach the oysters, onions, mushrooms, and parsley until the sides of the oysters curl, 1 to 2 minutes. Place the mixture in a blender and purée. Add the mixture to the broth. Add the milk, cream, and Tabasco and stir to combine.

Preheat oven to 350°F.

Cut the sheet of pastry dough into 8 squares. Pinch the corners of the dough to form baskets and bake until golden brown and puffed. When ready to serve, spoon the hot oyster mixture into the pastry shells and serve immediately.

Serves 6 to 8

Barbecued Oysters

Our use of the word "barbecue" for this dish is quirky at best. We're blending some aspects of barbecue sauce with some aspects of buffalo wing sauce.

SAUCE:

1/4 cup Crystal hot sauce or other Louisiana hot sauce

1/4 cup honey

1/4 cup loosely packed dark brown sugar

1 teaspoon orange zest

1 teaspoon lemon zest

COATING:

1 cup all-purpose flour

1 teaspoon salt

1 teaspoon freshly ground black pepper

1/2 teaspoon garlic powder

Vegetable oil for deep-frying

24 shucked oysters

⑥ To prepare the sauce, whisk together all of the ingredients over medium heat in a medium saucepan for 1 minute, or until the brown sugar is dissolved and hot. Remove the sauce from the heat and let cool at room temperature for at least 2 hours, or preferably overnight, to allow the flavors to mingle.

Reheat the sauce in a large skillet over medium heat. Heat the oil to 350°F. While the oil is heating, mix together all of the ingredients for the coating. Dredge the oysters in the coating, add them to the hot oil, and deep-fry until golden brown, about 2 minutes.

To serve, place the oysters in a large serving bowl. Serve the sauce in a separate bowl on the side for dipping, or lightly toss the oysters in the sauce.

Serves 6 to 8

Note: When preparing the zest of a citrus fruit, grate only the skin, not the bitter white pith. Zesting can be done with an official "zester," or with a vegetable peeler or paring knife.

Oyster-Spinach Pie

When I was growing up, I heard stories of the hardships endured by Croatian oystermen and their families during the Great Depression. They had absolutely no money to buy food—but they had lots of oysters. Oyster-Spinach Pie is an upgrade from those "no money" days.

TOPPING:

1 1/2 cups Italian-style bread crumbs

1 cup Romano cheese

2 tablespoons unsalted butter

2 tablespoons unsalted butter, at room temperature

1/2 cup chopped onions

1/2 cup chopped celery

1/2 cup chopped green bell peppers

3 dozen shucked oysters

1 1/2 teaspoons salt

2 teaspoons freshly ground black pepper

1 cup heavy whipping cream

1 cup milk

8 ounces cream cheese, at room temperature

1 1/2 teaspoons Tabasco sauce

2 cups chopped fresh spinach

1 cup pecorino Romano cheese

3 eggs, beaten

2 ready-made 8-inch pie crusts

⑥ To prepare the topping, put the bread crumbs, cheese, and butter in a large bowl. Cut together with a knife, like a streusel topping.

Preheat the oven to 350°F.

Melt the butter in a large pan. Add the onions, celery, and green peppers and sauté over medium-high heat, until the vegetables are soft. Add the oysters, salt, pepper, cream, and milk, stirring just until the oysters curl. Blend in the cream cheese and Tabasco with a spoon, followed by the spinach, cheese, and eggs.

Divide the filling between the pie crusts and bake in the oven until set, about 25 minutes. Remove the pies from the oven and sprinkle with the topping, then return the pies to the oven for 35 minutes, just until brown. Let cool to set, and serve.

Serves 8 to 10

Chilled Curried Oysters with Oriental Slaw

The flavors of several corners of the Far East come together in this fusion favorite. We taste India and Thailand in particular.

SLAW:

1/2 cup celery cut diagonally across rib

1/2 cup coarsely grated carrots

1/2 cup diced young green jackfruit or papaya

1/2 cup baby corn

2 tablespoons seasoned rice vinegar

1 tablespoon soy sauce

1/2 teaspoon chili paste

OYSTERS:

1 dozen shucked oysters

1 1/2 cups oyster water or clam juice

1 tablespoon curry powder

1/2 tablespoon granulated garlic

1/2 teaspoon ginger

1/4 teaspoon chili sauce

1 tablespoon cornstarch

1/4 cup water

ⓖ Mix slaw ingredients and chill.

In a medium saucepan, combine oysters, oyster water or clam juice, curry, garlic, and ginger. Over medium heat, poach the oysters until they curl. Remove the oysters and keep warm. Add chili sauce to the saucepan. Bring sauce to a boil and continue to cook until reduced by one third. In a small cup, dissolve cornstarch in water, then add to the saucepan.

In a large bowl, combine slaw, oysters, and chilled sauce.

Makes 4 appetizer servings

Oysters in Brown Garlic Sauce

Anytime something is called peasant food, it's likely to taste wonderful. We think of this dish as being inspired by the French countryside. In the city, it might turn up as rustic bistro fare.

BROWN GARLIC SAUCE:

1/2 cup oil

1/4 cup all-purpose flour

2 tablespoons chopped garlic

2 cups milk

1 cup oyster water or clam juice

4 tablespoons chopped green onions

1 tablespoon Worcestershire sauce

2 tablespoons parsley

1 teaspoon Tabasco sauce

1/4 teaspoon thyme

1/4 teaspoon black pepper

1/4 teaspoon salt

8 slices French bread, cut on the diagonal 3/4-inch thick
16 shucked oysters
1 cup cornmeal, seasoned with salt and pepper
Light vegetable oil for frying
Lemon wedges

⑥ In a medium saucepan, combine oil, flour, and garlic and cook over medium heat, stirring constantly, until roux is brown. Add remaining sauce ingredients. Do not allow sauce to boil.

Preheat oven to 400°F.

Arrange slices of French bread on a baking sheet and toast until brown, about 8 to 10 minutes.

Dredge oysters in a seasoned meal. Fry over high heat until brown on both sides, about 3 to 4 minutes per side. Place 2 slices of toasted bread on each plate. Top each with 2 oysters and 2 tablespoons of sauce. Garnish with lemon wedges.

Serves 4

Oyster Chicken Jambalaya

Here's an oyster-upgraded version of south Louisiana's famous rice dish, itself a New World spin on the paella that graces dining tables throughout Spain.

1 stick (1/4 pound) margarine
3 cups chopped onions
3 cups chopped celery
3 cups chopped peppers
24 shucked oysters
1 pound cooked chicken, diced
1 pound smoked sausage, thinly sliced
4 cups whole canned tomatoes
    (crushed with juice)
4 cups strong chicken stock
4 cups oyster water or clam juice
3 tablespoons Crystal hot sauce
1 tablespoon liquid smoke
3 teaspoons black pepper
3 teaspoons blackening spice
3 bay leaves
4 cups (2 pounds) rice

⑥ In a large skillet, over medium-high heat, sauté margarine, onions, celery, and peppers until onions are opaque. Add oysters, chicken, and sausage. Sauté until oysters curl, 3 to 4 minutes. Add remaining ingredients except rice. Bring to a boil. Add rice. Cover pot with a tight-fitting lid. Bring to a second boil. Remove from heat and let sit until rice absorbs all the liquid, 12 to 15 minutes. Fluff with a fork and serve hot.

Makes 10 to 12 servings

OUT OF AFRICA

In Togo and other sections of West Africa, oysters are usually pulled from the mangroves along the coast. The preferred recipe is dredging them in a peppery coating, deep-frying them, and rushing them to the hungry eaters, along with a super-spicy sauce on the side.

Spicy Sturgeon
with Artichoke Hearts, Spinach, Oysters, and Bell Pepper Sauce

You might call this recipe "Life after Caviar." It takes the huge, prehistoric sturgeon fish that gives the world its finest fish eggs, and really takes it for a fresh spin.

2 sweet red bell peppers
2 cups ice water
1 teaspoon Szechwan chili paste
1 teaspoon salt
1 tablespoon plus 2 teaspoons paprika
1 tablespoon ground black pepper
1 tablespoon ground white pepper
1 teaspoon ground cayenne pepper
1 teaspoon thyme leaves
2 teaspoons salt
2 8-ounce sturgeon fillets, skinned, or any
firm-fleshed white fish
3 tablespoons melted butter
1 cup white wine

1 teaspoon butter

3 ounces drained artichoke hearts, quartered

1/2 cup shucked oysters

1/2 cup oyster liquid

2 1/2 ounces fresh spinach, cleaned and deveined

⑥ Roast peppers over open flame until they are charred black. Plunge peppers in a bowl of ice water. Remove the skin, seeds, and stems. Place peppers in food processor, and purée. Add chili paste and salt and set aside.

Preheat oven to 350°F.

In a small bowl, mix paprika, black and white pepper, cayenne, thyme, and salt. Sprinkle sturgeon fillets generously with spice mixture. Melt butter and reserve in shallow bowl. Dredge sturgeon fillets in melted butter. Sauté sturgeon in a skillet over medium-high heat until brown on both sides. Transfer fillets to baking sheet. Pour butter from pan over fillets. Bake for 15 minutes.

Deglaze sauté pan with white wine, and continue to cook until reduced to $1/2$ cup. Remove from heat and reserve.

In a separate skillet, melt 1 teaspoon butter. Add artichoke hearts. Sauté until hot. Add oysters and oyster liquid. Continue to cook until almost no liquid remains. Add wine reduction and spinach. Toss gently until spinach is wilted and hot.

TO SERVE: On 2 plates, divide vegetable mixture. Top with sturgeon fillets. Top each fillet with 1 tablespoon bell pepper sauce. Serve immediately.

Makes 2 entrées

Panéed Oysters

The generous use of olive oil and seasoned breadcrumbs makes this a Mediterranean classic, with a special focus on Sicily.

1 1/2 cups Italian seasoned breadcrumbs
1 cup all-purpose flour
1 teaspoon finely ground black pepper
1/2 teaspoon salt
12 shucked oysters
1/2 cup olive oil, for frying
Grated Romano cheese

Mix all the dry ingredients together in a large bowl. Dredge oysters in the dry mixture. Heat olive oil in a saucepan. Fry oysters in 2 batches over high heat for 1 1/4 minutes on the first side and 45 seconds on the second side. Transfer oysters to a plate and sprinkle with 1 tablespoon of grated Romano cheese.

Serves 4

Filet Mignon Stuffed with Oysters

Here's a neat twist on the well-known fact that beef and oysters are terrific together, producing a sliceable and savory roll of the two main ingredients.

1 (10-ounce) filet mignon, cut against the
    grain into 4 equal pieces
Coarsely ground black pepper
16 shucked oysters
8 slices bacon
1 tablespoon brandy
1/2 cup heavy cream

⑥ Preheat oven to 350°F. Pound out filet mignon pieces. Sprinkle each with pepper. Place four oysters across each fillet and roll jellyroll style. Secure each end with a toothpick. Wrap 2 pieces of bacon end to end around each beef roll. Bake on small pan for 20 minutes. Turn and continue baking for 10 minutes. Set beef aside to rest.

Pour drippings into a small saucepan. Add 1 table-spoon brandy and set alight with a match. Add the 1/2 cup heavy cream and scrape the bottom of the saucepan.

Remove toothpicks from the beef rolls and slice each into 4 pieces. Divide the sauce evenly between 2 plates. Arrange 4 slices of beef roll around the sauce.

Serves 2

Fried Oyster Sandwich

In nineteenth-century New Orleans, this oyster sandwich was known as the "mediatrice," or peacemaker. When a husband fell out of favor with his wife or mistress, he simply brought her one of these.

COATING MIX:

1 cup cornmeal

1/2 cup white flour

1 teaspoon salt

1/2 teaspoon celery salt

1/2 teaspoon ground red pepper

1/2 teaspoon garlic powder

1/4 teaspoon ground allspice

Oil for frying

8 to 10-inch French baguette, sliced on the diagonal

Butter

8 to 12 shucked oysters per sandwich

Sliced dill pickles

Fresh lemon juice

⑥ In a medium mixing bowl, combine coating mix ingredients.

Heat oil in a large skillet to 350°F. Preheat oven to 350°F.

Roll oysters in the coating mix. Fry until golden brown, 3 to 4 minutes on each side. Drain on paper towels.

Butter both sides of bread slices. Place 8 to 12 oysters on one side and slices of dill pickle on the other side. Squeeze 1/2 of fresh lemon over the fried oysters. Close sandwich and place on baking sheet. Bake for about 5 minutes or until bread starts to brown.

Serves 2

Oyster Andouille Gumbo

The dark, roux-thickened soup or stew of the Gulf Coast gets an extra kick from the addition of oysters. Don't forget to reserve and pour in the oyster water, since it adds so much flavor.

2 pounds Andouille sausage, thinly sliced
2 cups and 3 tablespoons margarine
2 cups all-purpose flour
4 cups diced onions
4 cups diced celery
4 cups diced green peppers
2 cups dry sherry
4 large bay leaves
$1\frac{1}{2}$ gallons chicken stock
$\frac{1}{2}$ gallon (64 ounces) clam juice
5 tablespoons Worcestershire sauce
4 tablespoons Crystal hot sauce
2 tablespoons liquid smoke
2 tablespoons salt
1 tablespoon ground black pepper
1 tablespoon ground red pepper
1 tablespoon Tabasco sauce
4 tablespoons filé powder
36 shucked oysters and the oyster liquor (about 6 cups)

🌀 In a large stockpot, brown the andouille sausage. Remove sausage from the stockpot and set both aside.

In a medium skillet, melt 2 cups margarine and gradually stir in flour. Whisk over medium heat to produce a smooth, medium-brown roux. Arrest the cooking by stirring in some of the chopped vegetables and set aside.

Add the 3 tablespoons of margarine to the stockpot along with the rest of the onions, celery, and green peppers, stirring to scrape up brown bits of the sausage and continue to cook until the onions are opaque. Add all the other remaining ingredients except the oysters and filé powder. Bring to a boil and continue cooking until vegetables are soft, about 30 minutes. Add the roux gradually until the gumbo supports the vegetables in suspension and the boil becomes almost slow motion.

Add the oysters and andouille sausage. Cook 15 minutes. Serve over bowls of steamed rice.

Serves 8 to 10

Oyster Eggplant Casserole

Immigrants from Sicily brought over several variations on this casserole using eggplant, which they got from the Greeks, who in turn had borrowed it from the Turks.

1 large eggplant, peeled and cubed, about 2 cups
Salt
4 tablespoons extra virgin olive oil
1/2 cup chopped onions
1/2 cup chopped celery
1/2 cup chopped green peppers
1 teaspoon chopped garlic
1 slice of bacon, thinly sliced
1 1/2 cups oyster water or clam juice
2 cups stale French bread (soaked in water with excess water pressed out)
1 teaspoon Italian seasoning
1 teaspoon black pepper
1 tablespoon Crystal hot sauce
1 teaspoon lemon zest
24 shucked oysters
1 cup pecorino Romano cheese
2 tablespoons breadcrumbs

⑥ Place cubed eggplant in a medium stockpot. Cover with hot water and salt. Bring to a boil over high heat. Boil until tender, about 20 minutes.

Preheat oven to 375°F.

In a large saucepan, combine olive oil, onions, celery, green peppers, garlic, and bacon. Sauté, stirring constantly, for 5 to 6 minutes. Add 1 cup oyster water and the French bread. Cook until liquid is absorbed. Add 1/2 cup oyster water, Italian seasoning, black pepper, Crystal hot sauce, and lemon zest. Chop in oysters with spoon. Cook for about 10 minutes. Add salt, to taste and grated pecorino Romano cheese. Place into 4 small casserole dishes. Top with breadcrumbs. Bake until brown, about 15 minutes.

Makes 4 entrées

Oyster & Pork
in Lettuce Leaves

*Delicate Asian tastes and textures swirl
gently through these little lettuce pockets.
They're cool and they're crispy, making them
fine summer party food.*

Head of lettuce, large leaves pulled apart

1 pound coarsely ground pork

1 tablespoon sesame oil

1 tablespoon chopped garlic

1 can (8 ounces) water chestnuts, coarsely
   chopped

1/2 cup oyster water or clam juice

1 teaspoon dry mustard

1/2 teaspoon ground ginger

1 tablespoon seasoned rice vinegar

2 tablespoons dark soy sauce

2 tablespoons garlic chili paste

24 shucked oysters

1 tablespoon cornstarch

2 tablespoons water

3 green onions, thinly sliced

⑥ In a large skillet over high heat, sauté pork, sesame oil, garlic, and chestnuts until the pork is cooked through. Add oyster water, dry mustard, ginger, vinegar, soy sauce, and garlic chili paste. Cook for about 8 to 10 minutes. Add oysters. Cook until oysters curl.

In a small bowl, dissolve cornstarch in water. Add to the skillet. Add green onions and continue to cook until thick. Place 2 tablespoons of the mixture in the center of a lettuce leaf. Fold into an envelope and serve immediately.

Makes 10 to 12 appetizer servings

Artichokes with Creamy Oyster Sauce

This dish is all about eating something wonderful atop the leaves of fresh artichokes. You can cover the leaves with the sauce or, if you prefer, serve a bowl of sauce and plenty of leaves for dipping.

LOUIE SAUCE:

1/4 pound butter

1/2 cup white flour

4 ounces jumbo mushrooms, sliced

3 cups oyster water or clam juice

1 cup thinly sliced green onions

1/2 cup fresh chopped parsley

1/2 teaspoon thyme

2 teaspoons Tabasco sauce

1/2 cup white wine

1 tablespoon Worcestershire sauce

1 teaspoon black pepper

Salt to taste

24 shucked oysters

2 large artichokes

⑥ In a large skillet, melt butter over high heat. Whisk in flour. Add sliced mushrooms and stir for about 3 minutes. Stir in oyster water/clam juice. Add green onions and parsley. Cook for about 5 minutes. Add thyme, Tabasco, white wine, Worcestershire sauce and black pepper. Bring to a boil. Reduce heat and let simmer for about 15 minutes. Add salt to taste. Add oysters.

Clean artichokes. Cut each leaf a 1/4-inch to remove the thorny tip. Place in a stockpot with the stem-side down. Cover with water and bring to a boil over high heat. Cover and boil until tender, about 30 to 40 minutes. Cut each artichoke in half. Remove the choke (spiny thistles). Fan the artichoke half in bowl. Top with 6 oysters and 1 cup of Louie sauce.

Makes 4 servings

Oyster Spaghetti

When Croatians came to America around the turn of the century, many found themselves in their old Dalmatian Coast occupation—oystering. And whenever money was tight, they could invent some new way to eat the crop they'd harvested.

2 tablespoons extra virgin olive oil
1 tablespoon chopped garlic
1 cup chopped onions
1 tablespoon tomato paste
1 cup white wine
3 cups tomato sauce
2 cups chopped tomato
2 cups oyster water or clam juice
1 cup bottled clam juice
1 tablespoon oregano
1 teaspoon black pepper
1 tablespoon Worcestershire
1 teaspoon sugar
1/2 teaspoon Tabasco sauce
4 cups chopped oyster meat
1 cup chopped green onions
2 tablespoons chopped parsley

8 ounces pasta, cooked and drained
1/4 teaspoon salt
1/4 teaspoon pepper
Grated Romano cheese, for garnish

⑥ In a skillet, sauté garlic in oil over medium heat for one minute. Add onions and cook until translucent. Add tomato paste and cook, about 2 minutes. Add 1/4 cup of the white wine and mix well. Add tomato sauce and chopped tomatoes. Cook for 2 minutes. Add the remaining white wine. Increase heat to high until the mixture is boiling. Add oyster water or clam juice and bring to a boil. Continue to cook until the mixture is reduced by half, about 10 minutes. Add oregano, pepper, Tabasco, sugar, and Worcestershire. Reduce to a simmer. Add oyster meat, green onions and parsley. Cook for approximately 20 minutes. Remove from heat, set aside to cool, and refrigerate overnight.

TO ASSEMBLE: In a large sauté pan, place 1 cup of the oyster mixture over high heat. Add 1 cup cooked pasta with salt, pepper, and freshly grated Romano cheese, for garnish.

Pork Chops with Oyster Dressing

Pork is the meat of choice across the Deep South. Since oyster dressing is a coastal preference, we think of this holiday favorite as being from Charleston or perhaps Savannah.

ORANGE HONEY GLAZE:

3 tablespoons fresh orange juice
1/2 teaspoon orange zest
8 tablespoons honey
1/2 teaspoon Tabasco sauce
1/8 pound (1/2 stick) butter

OYSTER DRESSING:

1 loaf of stale French bread, cubed
6 cups water
3 tablespoons butter
1/2 cup diced green peppers
1/2 cup diced celery
1/2 cup diced onions
24 shucked oysters
1 cup oyster water or clam juice

1 teaspoon Tabasco sauce

1 teaspoon coarsely ground black pepper

1 teaspoon salt

1/2 teaspoon Worcestershire sauce

1/3 cup toasted pecans

1/3 cup green onions, diced

PORK LOIN CHOPS:

2 center cut loin chops, 1 1/2 pounds each

Salt and pepper to taste

⑥ In a medium saucepan, bring orange juice and orange zest to boil. Add honey and Tabasco and lower heat to a simmer. Whisk in butter. Remove from heat and reserve.

In a large bowl, soak French bread in water, then squeeze out as much as possible.

In a large skillet, melt butter, and sauté green peppers, celery, and onions until opaque. Add 2 cups of bread cubes, oysters, oyster water, Tabasco, coarse black pepper, salt, and Worcestershire sauce. Continue to cook until liquid is reduced by half. Combine with pecan pieces and green onions.

Preheat oven to 350°F.

Cut the large half of each loin chop to the bone, butterflying each chop. Salt and pepper to taste. Place each loin chop on a baking sheet and bake for approximately 5 minutes. Glaze with orange honey glaze. Cook until done, 5 to 7 more minutes.

TO ASSEMBLE: Center a generous portion of oyster dressing onto each plate. Place the loin chop, butterfly-side down, on top of the dressing. Drizzle orange honey glaze over the loin chop. Garnish with roasted pecans.

Serves 4 to 6

Also from the authors of *OYSTERS*

CONVERSIONS

LIQUID

1 tablespoon = 15 milliliters
1/2 cup = 4 fluid ounces = 125 milliliters
1 cup = 8 fluid ounces = 250 milliliters

DRY

1/4 cup = 4 tablespoons = 2 ounces = 60 grams
1 cup = 1/2 pound = 8 ounces = 250 grams

FLOUR

1/2 cup = 60 grams
1 cup = 4 ounces = 125 grams

TEMPERATURE

400 degrees F = 200 degrees C = gas mark 6
375 degrees F = 190 degrees C = gas mark 5
350 degrees F = 175 degrees C = gas mark 4

MISCELLANEOUS

2 tablespoons butter = 1 ounce = 30 grams
1 inch = 2.5 centimeters
all purpose flour = plain flour
baking soda = bicarbonate of soda
brown sugar = demerara sugar
confectioners' sugar = icing sugar
heavy cream = double cream
molasses = black treacle
raisins = sultanas
rolled oats = oat flakes
semisweet chocolate = plain chocolate
sugar = caster sugar